EAGLE THE FLYING HUNTER

Nancy Lazarus

In the heat of summer, on a cloudy and dull day, in the chill of winter, on a lovely spring day, and in autumn, when the trees are bare, the eagle flies up and down gliding in the wind, high up in the sky hunting for his meal. He spreads out his wings like an aeroplane and glides up and down below the clouds, cutting through the air with his strong wings, whoop, whoop, as he soars to the north, south, west and east. His strong sharp talons always stretch out ready to lift his prey. His strong thick beak is ready to tear his meat meal into pieces.

The Eagle is a flying hunter.

As he flies, the eagle always looks deep down to the ground with his sharp eyes searching deeply between the blades of grasses, through the leaves of bushy shrubs and trees, in the forest, in the valleys, on mountain tops and slopes, looking for anything that moves.

The hungry eagle must catch one of the little creatures for his lunch. He wants something meaty like a lizard or a large worm for breakfast, a baby rabbit for lunch, and a little bird, a snake or a mouse for his afternoon snack! When he is very hungry and when he has a little nestling in his nest high up in the trees to feed, then he must make a good catch.

The eagle whistles as he flies. The wind too whistles through his wings.

When all the little creatures see the eagle's shadow as he flies past, they tremble with fear and rush to hide.

The little wrens that usually leap and hop from one thick grass stem to another chirp, chirping and picking grass seeds with their tiny but strong beaks near the pond freeze into a dead silence with fear when the eagle flies past.

When the dark shadow quickly flashes over them they warn each other of the danger coming.

"Sh-sh-sh! Quiet everyone! The eagle, the eagle is here." The little birds whisper to each other to stop chirping.

"Are you sure it him?" One of the little birds asks.

"It is him, the big strong hungry eagle flying high in the sky, I heard his whistle, I saw his shadow!" One clever little bird tells her friends.

"It can't be", says another, "that was a black stalk!".

The clever little bird warns her friends.

"Stop talking and do as I say! Everyone kneel down and put your head to the ground! Don't move and don't shake the grass! Let the eagle fly on! He must not catch one of us. He must not see us!"

The little birds lye flat on the ground their little hearts pounding hard through their little chests and fine feathers, boom! boom! boom! The eagle flies in a circle but does not see the birds. He turns and flies lower than before.

His hungry eyes search once more but he cannot see anything moving. He has nothing to eat for lunch.

The lizard hears the eagle whistle and pushes himself under dry leaves on the ground.

"The eagle must not catch me." The lizard mumbles softly to himself, his little nose sweating with fear, his long tail flat on the ground like a dry lifeless stick.

Mother rabbit hurries her baby rabbits under the leafy shrub.

"Shew! Rush under the bush and tuck your heads between your front legs! Don't move!"

Her legs are shaking with fear.

"The eagle should never see my babies!" Mother rabbit whispers to herself gritting her big front teeth as she too hides under the shrub, her large ears flat on her back, her eyes half open and watching on her babies.

The snake hurries for his life. He slides and slithers fast on the grass like an electric train heading home, into the dark hole under the big log, eyes wide open with fear. "The eagle can't have me for his lunch! I will run for my life!"

Mother mouse is gathering grass to make a comfortable bed for her little ones. She sees the eagle's shadow and quickly tucks herself under the bundle of grass she has gathered.

"I will stay here until he goes!" The mouse whispers to herself as she pushes herself under the grass, her long tail stretched out like a dry stick. She too is shaking with fear.

The eagle fails to catch something in the valley today. He whistles with anger. "Wee---woo!" He flaps his strong wings and flies away.

The little birds sigh with relief.

"Wow! That was close! He is gone for now! We can relax!"

The little birds tell each other.

The birds stretch their little legs and wings and carry on looking for food.

The rabbit family relaxes too.

The snake peers out through the hole. He is not in a hurry to come out.

"I will rest a while before I go out again. Maybe a frog may hop past or a mouse can come by. I could be lucky and have a good lunch."

The snake licks his mouth with his long forked tongue.

The mouse gathers her bundle of grass and nips to her home.

"Let me hurry home, my children are hungry!"

The lizard shakes off the leaves from his back and crawls to the nearby rock to bask in the sun.

"Let me enjoy the warmth of the sun for now!" The lizard stretches himself lazily on the rock.

The eagle flies to the tall shady tree in the middle of the forest. He will wait there for some time then goes out again to hunt.